# RENAISSANCE

Troll Associates

# RENAISSANCE

by Francene Sabin
Illustrated by Hal Frenck

**Troll Associates**

*Library of Congress Cataloging in Publication Data*

Sabin, Francene.
    Renaissance.

    Summary: Briefly traces developments in European
art, architecture, music, literature, philosophy,
science, and exploration between 1300 and 1600.
    1. Renaissance—Juvenile literature.  [1. Renais-
sance.  2. Europe—History.  3. Civilization, Modern]
I. Frenck, Hal, ill.  II. Title.
CB361.S29    1985        940.2 '1        84-2695
ISBN 0-8167-0246-2 (lib. bdg.)
ISBN 0-8167-0247-0 (pbk.)

When the mighty Roman Empire fell, about 1,500 years ago, it left a weak and divided Europe. Trade and commerce almost disappeared, travel became dangerous, and the arts and culture went into a decline. The great cities began to decay, and the magnificent monuments and highways of the Empire were left to crumble.

Europe turned into a vast expanse of feudal estates, ruled by warlike nobles and worked by peasants. Life in the Middle Ages was poor, brief, and cruel for most people. There was little time for art or culture. In fact, art and culture would have died out completely if it had not been for the church.

Learning was kept alive in the monasteries. Priests taught reading and writing. Fine cathedrals were built all over Europe. They were decorated with statues of saints and with stained-glass windows showing scenes from the Bible. The music of the time was church music, and the books were hand-copied works of religion.

In time, trade and travel returned to Europe, cities and towns were built up again, and feudalism grew weak. Many events caused these changes.

The years of the plague, called the Black Death, left many feudal estates unpopulated. The crusaders returned from the East carrying new treasures and filled with new ideas. A growing middle class of merchants and skilled craftsmen began to support kings instead of feudal lords. As feudalism died, the Middle Ages drew to a close in Europe. A new age—the Renaissance—was born.

The *Renaissance*, which means "rebirth," brought tremendous advances in art, architecture, music, literature, philosophy, science, and exploration. And these advances, during the three centuries from 1300 to 1600, laid the foundation for the modern world.

The Renaissance began with a renewed interest in the culture of the ancient world. Greek and Roman art and the literature of the past were studied and copied. This led to a rebirth of a philosophy called humanism. Humanism stresses the dignity and worth of human beings and of human interests, instead of only church interests.

Humanism took many forms during the Renaissance. Artists created paintings of kings and common people, of landscapes, and of scenes from mythology—instead of only religious subjects.

Architects began to design palaces, homes for the wealthy, and buildings for government—instead of only cathedrals. Writers now wrote love poetry, political essays, historical plays, and comedies—works that had little or nothing to do with the church. And in music, Renaissance composers wrote songs and compositions for rich patrons, instead of only church music.

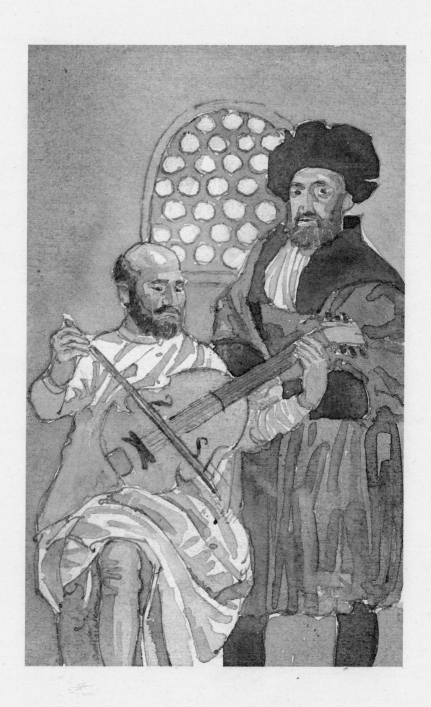

Italy is often called the birthplace of the Renaissance. There were several reasons for this. Chief among them was Italy's geographical location.

Italy is located on the Mediterranean Sea, closer to the East than any other European country. As trade with the East increased in the late Middle Ages, Italian cities grew rich. As a result, the merchants and princes in these cities were able to pay for handsome homes, fine paintings, and other works of art. They became patrons of the arts.

Italy also possessed a great treasure of
ancient Greek and Roman art and literature.
There were ruins of classical temples and
grand homes; there were statues and magnificent wall paintings; there were manu-
scripts of ancient poetry, plays, and essays.
These works of art had been gathered during
the Roman Empire, more than 1,000 years
before, and they were the basis of the new
interest in the classical period.

In Italy, the church also contributed to the Renaissance. For example, the church hired the best painters, sculptors, and architects to build and decorate Vatican City in Rome. Vatican City is the seat of the Roman Catholic Church and the home of the Pope. During the Renaissance, Vatican City became a magnificent center of art and architecture.

The greatest Renaissance masters worked for the church. Michelangelo painted the walls and ceiling of the Sistine Chapel and designed the dome for St. Peter's Church.

He also fashioned marvelous sculptures, such as the *Pietà*, for the Vatican. Many other artists, such as Giotto, Botticelli, Raphael, and Leonardo da Vinci created masterpieces for the church.

During the Renaissance, the classical writings of Greece and Rome were rediscovered. Moreover, literature began to appear in the *vernacular*, which means the language spoken by the people. Using the vernacular in writing was a complete change from the past, when everything was written in Latin—the language of the church.

*The Decameron*, by Giovanni Boccaccio, is one of the outstanding examples of Italian Renaissance literature. It is a series of entertaining stories told by a group of nobles who have escaped from a city struck by the plague.

The use of the vernacular in literature was even more important in Northern Europe, because in England, France, and the Germanic countries, the vernacular was strongly tied to a sense of nationalism.

Literature written in English obviously had a stronger effect on English-speaking people than anything written in Latin. French literature likewise meant much more to the French-speaking people. The use of the

vernacular was very effective. In Germany the vernacular was part of a rebellion against the Church of Rome. One of the strongest voices in this movement was Martin Luther.

Martin Luther was a German priest who felt that the church should be reformed. Luther wanted the church to be closer to the people. He wanted to allow prayer in the vernacular, instead of only in Latin. He also wanted the church to give up much of its ceremony and emphasis on wealth. While he was devoutly religious, Luther was in many ways a humanist. He believed that every person was equal before God.

From the teachings of Luther—as well as those of John Calvin of Switzerland, John Knox of Scotland, and other reformers— came the Protestant faiths and the movement known as the Reformation.

The forces of Protestantism, humanism, and nationalism all worked together during the Reformation to loosen the hold of the Catholic Church on Europe, particularly in the northern countries.

Modern science and technology also had their beginnings during the Renaissance, dramatically changing the way people saw the world around them. One of the most dramatic changes came with the invention of the printing press. Until Johannes Gutenberg, of Germany, invented movable type in the middle of the fifteenth century, all printing was done by hand.

Hand-printing made books very rare and expensive. They limited reading to the very rich, a tiny percentage of the population. But Gutenberg's invention made books more available and less expensive. As a result, more and more people learned to read.

The Renaissance also saw remarkable advances in medicine. Girolamo Fracastoro, famous for his studies of contagious diseases, was the first doctor to identify typhus. Before Fracastoro and other medical pioneers of the Renaissance, disease was considered a punishment sent by God. The workings of the human body were thought to be unsolvable mysteries.

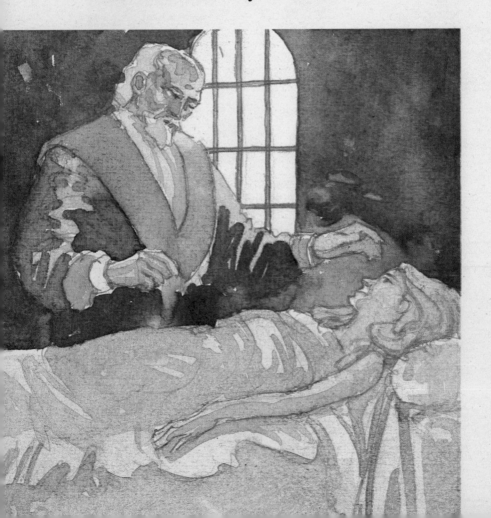

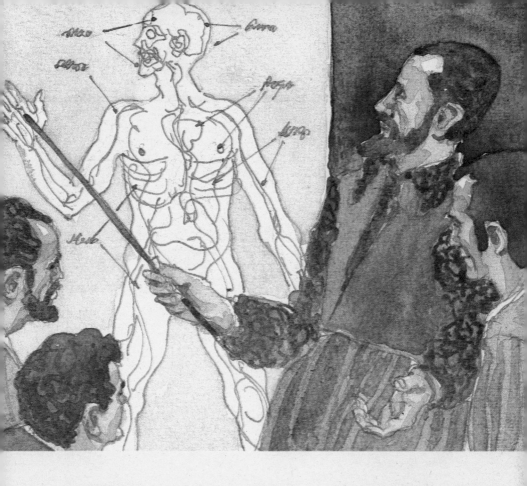

Others in the forefront of Renaissance medicine were a Swiss physician called Philippus Paracelsus and a Belgian doctor named Andreas Vesalius. Paracelsus was a pioneer in clinical studies of diseases and in the use of chemicals to treat disease. Vesalius is known as the "father of anatomy" for his extensive work in the study of the human body.

Modern astronomy also began during the Renaissance. It started with the work of Nicolaus Copernicus, a Polish scientist. Copernicus showed, by mathematics and logic, that the Earth and the planets revolve around the sun.

This theory was given further proof by Galileo Galilei, an Italian astronomer. Galileo, using a telescope to observe the night sky, discovered that Jupiter has moons revolving around it. He also discovered that Venus goes through phases as it circles the sun, just as our moon goes through phases as it circles the Earth. The work of these two scientists destroyed forever the idea that the Earth was the center of the universe.

Along with astronomy and medicine, map-making advanced swiftly with the work of Gerhard Mercator. Map-making was very important during this period because this was also the age of exploration.

Explorers, such as Christopher Columbus, Ferdinand Magellan, Amerigo Vespucci, John Cabot, Sir Francis Drake, and Jacques Cartier, were as much a part of the Renaissance as the creative geniuses Leonardo da Vinci, William Shakespeare, and Miguel Cervantes.

Many new worlds were opened during the Renaissance. They were the worlds of art and science, of education and medicine, of religion and philosophy, and of music and literature. And new horizons were extended far beyond the bounds of Europe, as sailing ships reached the shores of the New World. A new age was beginning, built on the strides taken by the giants of the Renaissance.